RACHEL PINK

BALBOA.PRESS
A DIVISION OF HAY HOUSE

Copyright © 2020 Rachel Pink.

All rights reserved. No part of this book may be used or reproduced by any means, graphic, electronic, or mechanical, including photocopying, recording, taping or by any information storage retrieval system without the written permission of the author except in the case of brief quotations embodied in critical articles and reviews.

Balboa Press books may be ordered through booksellers or by contacting:

Balboa Press
A Division of Hay House
1663 Liberty Drive
Bloomington, IN 47403
www.balboapress.com
1 (877) 407-4847

Because of the dynamic nature of the Internet, any web addresses or links contained in this book may have changed since publication and may no longer be valid. The views expressed in this work are solely those of the author and do not necessarily reflect the views of the publisher, and the publisher hereby disclaims any responsibility for them.

The author of this book does not dispense medical advice or prescribe the use of any technique as a form of treatment for physical, emotional, or medical problems without the advice of a physician, either directly or indirectly. The intent of the author is only to offer information of a general nature to help you in your quest for emotional and spiritual well-being. In the event you use any of the information in this book for yourself, which is your constitutional right, the author and the publisher assume no responsibility for your actions.

Any people depicted in stock imagery provided by Getty Images are models, and such images are being used for illustrative purposes only. Certain stock imagery © Getty Images.

Print information available on the last page.

ISBN: 978-1-9822-3852-0 (sc)
ISBN: 978-1-9822-3853-7 (e)

Balboa Press rev. date: 12/16/2019

Foreword

I almost hope you will skip reading this foreword, as It's all about me! I truly believe now that these poems are for you, out there. They may speak to you and for you or those that you know. You can dip in and out as you wish, open a page and see what's there for you. Expressions touch and move us all in different very unique ways. I hope you get something from them.

I first started to write poems in my childhood; to express externally, some of the pain, confusion and craziness of life. I think I was born with a melancholy heart and soul, as so many artists throughout time have been, yet create such wonders through their torment. As an adolescent I felt so much emotional and mental pain I thought I couldn't make it through life. Struggling with a myriad of mental and emotional health difficulties, at times becoming almost translucent to myself, hiding it all from the world with innocent smiles and quietness, staying below radar in my family, appearing to be the one no-one needed to 'worry about'. My writings were a friend, council and true release. Often explaining to me what I was feeling and how I was coping. Sometimes they would purely be an expression. On occasion, as I grew up, they would be an ego inflation, like a best friend fluffing your feathers when you're feeling down. It's some of these that I love to read over and over…. The superior arrogance amuses me; a penned masquerade! Over time these have become a magical crutch reminding me of my power.

Most poems pop up from no-where and they can be gone just as fast. Some tease me with gestures but don't allow me to complete them, like feeling the essence of a dream that you can't grasp for long enough to remember or explain. Some linger and bug me for days until I put ink to paper. Mostly though, they go SPLAT 'here I am… these are some of your internal bits; get me quick or else I'm gone!'

Some-times I burst with the desire and need to grab a pen and anything to write on, so I don't lose the words that need to spill out of me, cleansing me like a warm fresh shower.

I don't adhere to the rules of poetry and no longer feel the need to hide my expressions for fear of being judged on the intellectual content, phrasing or context; a flow of anything should be allowed to flow without restriction!

Over time, as life seems to share many sorrows with me; these poems may seem like they're not going to end on an up-beat note, which I truly desire. I have been on such journeys of self and world discoveries. Seeking a happier soul, thinking I have solved life's problems, learnt all my lessons only to find my-self in another predicament and my soul in howling pain again. Learning, learning the hardest way, the only way! Then when I was 36, the worst thing happened, my baby son died. I tried to work through my pain, and I did write but the pain was and still is so indescribable that I would often just scream onto the paper 'AAAAHHHHHHHH' for page after page after page. Understanding that I am one of those people who *appear* to hold it together in-front of others; quiet and polite, a people pleaser and not one to make a scene; I could wish to be like the wailing women in Italian funerals as I'm sure it's an incredibly healthy thing to be able to release pain so loudly and openly, but I'm now such a believer in being true to one's self and never forcing yourself, whom ever you may be, to be as others think you should or how society 'expects' you to be. Be you and I'll be me.

I laugh a lot again now, my loving partner in life and I have the most beautiful daughter who is such a powerful force in this world. I feel joy and like to offer joy and counsel to those around me or in need! But inside I will forever scream in pain for the loss of my beautiful boy.

Life in all its glory and cruelty keeps reminding me that happiness, love and joy come at a price, that price is pain, for when we care and love, we feel, when we feel, we are wide open to hurt!! Grief is one of the most incredibly 'real' things anyone can feel. Never had I felt so utterly connected to nature, I was levelled. I was as one with any elephant not able to leave their dead calf or penguin mother ushered away by other kind penguins to say goodbye to their baby who had died. Why should I be any more special than them! I had to say goodbye and leave my tiny baby behind and carry on in this world because this world carries on.

But I shall continue to shine light through all pain, holding it compassionately with kindness and care. So many of us struggle through this life, many of us carrying grief and pain silently, allowing those moments of sunshine and rainbows, synchronicity and smiles to brighten your day and *remind you of what's truly important… You're here!… on glorious planet earth! It's amazing and full of magic, love, joy and happiness; as well as the tough stuff that makes the wonderful all the more real … We need to take far better care for our glorious planet and each other and it all starts on a very intimate, individual level. When and if you can, as often as you can, enjoy, love and laugh with true respect and care. These are gifts to your own soul, your loved ones and the wider world as they ripple out.*

I hope you enjoy my words inspired by my journey.

Somewhere between self and creation, imagination blooms. Ignited by passion, drawn on through desire. Truly a great distinguishable trait us humans should be proud of!

Gratitude's!

I give thanks to all of those I have crossed paths with over my life. For better or worse you have added to my glorious tapestry. Particularly though, my close supportive family and friends who showed themselves with truth through darkness and offered unending support; you may never know how much you mean to me.
To my mum whose energy and vitality know no bounds with a laugh that brings light into any room. My brother James who's fountain of knowledge flows over, who's always been there for me as gentle support and a wackiness to make me laugh.
To my wonderful Carl and Amelie who keep the wind beneath my wings and a joyful song in my heart.

Contents

Foreword v

The Beginning 1
    Scrambled 3
    Original sin 4
    Island 5
    Lonely Lake 6
    All and Everything 7
    Nature 8

Awakening 9
    Dawn 11
    Snowflake 12
    Find You 13
    Starburst (Song) 14
    Universe 16
    Goddess 17
    Windowsill 18

A Journey 19
    Breathe Again 21
    Free as a Bird (song) 22
    Angels 24
    Yoga 26
    Magnetism 27
    Tears in Waterfalls (song) 28

Slipping Illusions 31
    World on My Finger 33
    Violin Man 34
    Life 35
    Warbled 36

  Heartbreak 37
  Lost Dream 38

Beyond the Dream 39
  Realise it's Alright (Song) 41
  Cradled in the Arms of Destiny 42
  Eternal Motion 43
  Autumns Hour 44
  Young Girl 45

The Wish 47
  Destiny Walks in Your Hand 49
  Dark Fairy 50
  Clouds Fulfil Dreams 51
  Warrior and Poet 52

Balance in Darkness 53
  Our boy is lost 55
  The Drama 56
  Love 57
  Beautiful Hands We Share 58
  Do Not Compare! 60

Forward Motion 61
  Goddess 2014 63
  Wonderful Hero 64
  Amelie 66
  Ripple 67
  Sunday Breakfast 68
  Symmetry 69

Final Note 71

The Beginning

Scrambled

The pain of the noise,
Is like the loneliness of hell,
Knotting insides with tears,
Helplessness.

Screaming silently,
Like a dream;
Speaking the words in thought.
Carrying on in an unsuppressed world;
The world that suppresses us all.

Fighting the anger,
Turning another page.

As darkness falls,
Who knows the colours?
In life,
Who knows the game?

Ignorance is our saviour,
As living is our death.
Yet as the saying goes,
We save the best till last.

Feelings which are scrambled,
Ignored by thought,
Like personality,
Ignored by touch.

Is your life reality?
Do you live in a dream?
If you do,
Is your dream reality?
Or reality, just your dream!

Age 15

Original sin

I was sleeping in my bed
when I heard her cry,
which broke my dream
and brought me life.

In the morning
her beautiful face was black and blue
A ridge round her neck
where her chain had been strung;

I did not pay attention to this
For I was only young.

But as I grew up, I began to hate!
Whether it was myself or him
I did not know.

But it's my fault this happened
I came into this world and now I must pay,
Many heart breaks and sorrow come my way.

So, who do I have left?
No one, I think,
Though many say they love me.

What do they love?
Not me, for I seem strange to people
Dormant and weak;

So, who do I have left?
Only me!

Age 16

Island

Island,
A million miles away,
In the middle of the ocean.

Island, full of promise,
And extinction,
Where, lowly flowers bloom,

Full of colour and scent,
But die alone and desolate,
In winter rains.

Waterfalls that flow with tears,
From the darkest skies,
Washing into oceans depths.

Sands caressed gently,
Air filled with fragrance;
An indescribable longing to wash away in tenderness.

Moon shining bright,
Reflects on seas of loneliness;
This island, a million miles away.

Age 16

Lonely Lake

Lonely lake,
With endless depths,
And stagnant solitude,
Aching to seep through porous stone.

Heart, dead:
Lying cold, motionless inside
A body that remains a shell.
Loneliness embellishes each particle.

'Capable of love', words in jest!
None so frozen can withstand.
Dead to know love,
And for love to know.

Hidden, are a million truths;
A thousand lies, told.
Too much felt, soul torn,
Too deep to surface.

Is love, possible,
In clarities blossom?!
Pain yet pours the only way;
Torture of a heart that should lie cold.

Lonely lake,
With endless depth,
And stagnant solitude,
Aching to seep through porous stone.

Age 18

All and Everything

I am in love;
A love that consumes me,
The love of fear and longing,
A love that empowers to disable.

A love of all lost loves,
For to be me, alone,
Is the greatest freedom,
The purest heart.

I can be untouched,
Yet seem to bewitch,
Through my want to be alone,
Not fixed or squashed.

I am a Goddess,
High in the clouds,
Lost in thought and deep contemplation,
Saddened to be demonised in this way.

Challenge not,
The goals cannot be scored,
I don't need to be 'we'.
I am the all, the everything.

Leave me be;
Don't try any more,
And, if as a crone,
I am still alone,

That will be my will,
My want, sadness or joy.
Dispel your pity,
I am the all, the everything.

Age 24

Nature

Sometimes when I hear the wind,
I hear a voice I do not know.
Through the rustle of the trees,
Leaves suspended mid-air,
By a strand of invisible web,

Nature engulfs me.
My breath entwined in air,
Softly, freedom emerges from my soul,
Submersed in a moment.

Catatonic life,
Still with power and energy,
Taken up through the trees,
Bound, temporarily, in the body of the web.

Calmed with peace,
Beauty never known unless seen,
The voice is heard,
No, felt.

In the form of a wave,
Washing through me, in me.
Tones of Tidal motion,
Feeling it is everywhere.

Chiming, glorious blues,
The voice is reason, meaning.
Welcoming tone, never to explain.
And it comes from within me, it is me,
I am free.

Age 26

Awakening

Dawn

The dawn is beauty unsurpassed,
Her wet lips and cool breath,
Caress every particle of air.

Filtered through misty glaze,
Haze that swims round erected concrete,
Yet soft to touch a blade of grass.

When all is quiet and new,
Only a bird's melodic song
Can break the infectious silence.

I would stand all night
To baptise myself in morning dew;
To feel the wetness of tranquillity,

And start anew.   *Age 26*

Snowflake

A snowflake
Falling, through blackened sky;
Shimmering silver,
Encapsulated in its' own time.

In its four-dimensional state
It is alone;
Ever floating on thermals of space,
Its beauty intensifies.

Softer than imaginable,
So delicate in its individuality;
Destructively fragile in a breeze,
Yet more complex than you could believe.

It would fall forever
Through calming skies;
Glowing with its lonely beauty,
From the depths of its frozen heart.

But the skies can never be still,
There is always at least a breeze,
And always a storm brewing.
A snowflake cannot know its destiny.

Age 26

Find You

Settle in peace,
And let thy drift,
Gently through this mist.
Feel comfort, as I speak,
And let me caress you,
As you relax.

Gentle heat, drifts,
Upon gentle winds.
You wonder, will this last?
Hear me,
With only sweetness and serenity,
Hear me though you pass.

Your conscious mind
Is now you not,
You can now think true.
Though not asleep,
But not awake,
Just explore and find you.

Age 21

Starburst (Song)

A star bursts in the dark,
Shattering space,
Clouds lit like candy floss,
Covered in lace.

I saw the look of an angel,
Was he you?
Are you watching me right now?

Moon lighting the cosmos,
Everything is new,
Entangled in hope,
Come in and share my mind.

Dreaming on my own,
To find your face,
Drinking fluid from this space:

Are you here?
Are you there?
Are you watching me right now?

Illuminating beauty,
Captured in fate,
Iridescent colours,
Alive and awake.

The universe is crying;
I can feel her pain,
Come in and share my mind,
Drown in her tears,
Feel the power from beneath.

You taught me everything,
Are you here?
Are you watching me right now?   *Age 27*

Universe

I sit on the edge of the universe,
Dangling my feet in the stars,
Rippling the space with my toes.

I design the constellations,
I light up all the moons,
I transcend time.

The Earth is as a marble,
Small & delicate in its glassy beauty,
Balancing precariously in time.

Planetary alignment,
Mistaken or misjudged?
It is just my game.

Your silly thing called life,
Existence is just a blink in my time;
It's all just to keep me amused!

So, I sit on the edge of the universe,
Dangling my feet in the stars;
Rippling the space with my toes.

Age 28

Goddess

I am a Goddess,
I shine and exude light,
I struggle with my supreme existence;

I am tested,
As all Goddesses are;
I am shown the way through struggle.

I've been pained in many ways:
Bound, chastised,
Ridiculed and demonised.

And, I stand here;
Edged on a precipice,
Scared beyond my wits.

Yet my fear will not hold me,
I am after all a goddess;
I will embrace my fear.

I will make a new path,
For the one I have followed
Seems to be cursed.

I relinquish myself.
Let the universe attack me,
And I will open my heart and love;

I will stand tall,
Illuminate all I feel,
I will be me.

Age 28

Windowsill

*Where is this indecision
found on a windowsill,
I do not dare to dream,
of a life without the view of Nottingham
can it be seen?*

*A place so full of hope and dread,
A place that offered me shelter
When I thought I could be dead.
I do not dare to dream!*

*Yet dream I must,
lest my dreams of me,
turn to dust.*

*Too late in the day to hide and cry.
There could be something else that's passing me by.*

*This life, we're told, is too short;
and if it passes cunningly,
to ignore every thought, would be to abort all the possibilities open to me.*

*So, there is this indecision found on a windowsill,
I am beginning to dream
of a life without the view of Nottingham;
I believe it can be seen.*   *Age 27*

A Journey

Breathe Again

Only tranquillity can come from an empty mind.
Silence your thoughts for now.
Find peace and enlightenment.
Float your mind in calm waters,
Absorb the energy from still.

Remember,
This life is a gift!
Open your eyes,
Breathe again.

Wherever you are,
You can live!
Just remember to appreciate,
Everything!

Know true beauty,
And you will see it everywhere,
And smile.

Open yourself,
Find the higher state,
It is then you will truly understand,
It's all there and always has been.
Open your eyes.
Breathe again. *Age 28*

Free as a Bird (song)

I woke up early one morning,
With tear drops falling down my face,
And I said to my-self, baby,
It's time to get some release.

See I'd been falling through my existence,
Bored, frightened and alone,
And I realised that fateful morning,
It was time to get me out of the stinking hole.

Cause I wanted to be,
Free, as a bird.
One foot in front of the other,
Soaring high,
Eyes open to discover.

I got my-self a ticket,
I packed myself a bag,
Before I even knew it,
I was flying out of town.

I flew over the ocean,
To the other side of the world,
Wanted to have myself some adventure,
Wanted to mend my broken soul.

And I started to be,
Free, as a bird,
One foot in front of the other,
Soaring high,
Mind open to discover.

These shoes I've tramped in,
Memories carved out in the soul,
Seeing things, I've only dreamed of,
Mending my broken soul.

Practising new teachings,
with every corner that I turn.
Crossing another ocean,
Stepping out into a brand-new dawn.

And now I am,
Free, as a bird,
One foot in front of the other,
Soaring high,
So much yet to discover.

And let me tell you baby,
Let me tell you what I saw;
I saw my reflection standing beside me,
Showing me, I could make it on my own.

And now I am
Free as a bird,
And I'm standing free

The poet, the goddess, the artist
Standing free.

I'm free as a bird,
One foot in front of the other,
Soaring high….
So much yet to discover.

Free as a bird. *Age 28*

Angels

With angels of beauty and dragons of power,
The brightness the greens that dazzle with light.
The calmness the stillness the open support,
Comes' only the energy from the moon.

The sound of the ocean,
The sunsets astounding,
If angels were earthly,
This place is where they'd dance,
These are the skies the dragons set alight.

There's an energy surrounding me,
A light that absorbs me,
In movement and breathing,
Feet lost in a dance.

The earth is calling,
I lend her my rhythm,
She's giving, she's breathing,
We live in her wonder.
Sound and motion percolate my soul.

Eyes wide open to a much larger picture.
Experiences are had through the eyes of a child.
Kinship from all corners, explosions of laughter,
Maybe the sound of angels' song.

Fly all Angels', not just ones unearthly,
For this is our chance to expand the journey.

Sing songs, tell stories,
Speak true of cultures.
Bang your feet on the floor in celebration and dance,
Build new ways to bridge the gaps.

Enlighten your mind and share in your gain.
Live in excitement;
Open your eyes in wonder,
This is a place, where some angels I know dance.   *Age 28*

Yoga

Right here,
In this moment,
Where all resides.

On this breath,
Is my life,
That I shall ride.

Elongating every moment,
For it is the first.
Knowing nothing,

Just me,
Just you,
The universe.

Pure love,
One time,
In this moment;
Shine.

Age 28

Magnetism

Come, let us dance in the moonlight,
Whilst black crystal waters
Crash in a crescendo.
As our lips meet and our souls entwine,
Drawn into the universe.
Soaring through distant galaxies,
Our bodies merge.
Like the shores enveloped,
By each wave drawing sands deep;
Moving as tides,
Drawn by the magnetism of the moon.
At one with everything,
Our bodies alone.

Age 28

Tears in Waterfalls (song)

Tears in waterfalls;
Face like rocks etched in space,
Where my life is gushing down,
In memories of the past.

People and places, said goodbye,
I'm reminded of my dreams;
In living, they seem to last.

Tears in waterfalls,
Tears in waterfalls,
Tears in waterfalls.

Birds calling souls, from another life;
Singing past loneliness,
Knowing future song.

Releasing memories, captured in a spider's web,
Now floating with pure ease,
Releasing all the pain.

Tears in waterfalls,
Tears in waterfalls,
Tears in waterfalls.

Releasing all the pain,
Absorbed through each grain,
Cascading through the earth;
Releasing all the pain.

Tears in waterfalls,
I cry my pain away,
In tears in waterfalls,
Tears in waterfalls.

Tears in waterfalls;
Face like rocks etched in space,
Where my life is gushing down,
I find peace.

In tears in waterfalls. *Age 28*

Slipping Illusions

World on My Finger

I found the world,
Wore it on my finger.
Though bound in silver,
The world kept pushing free.
Each time, found
In a mysterious way
But I knew it needed to be free.
'To stick it,' I thought, trap it from its path!
Yet the world thwarted my plans,
And leapt free into grassy sands!
Though I searched and reached,
The world didn't come back to be worn on my finger.
All the while, I would linger on the thought...
But now I know,
That by letting go...
I don't need to wear the world on my finger,
I can wear it in my heart.

Age 29

Violin Man

Lonely violin man,
Telling many a sad story,
Of a life unknown to me.
Play to moving present,
A populous undeserved.
Those strings and bow,
Crying and swimming,
Carving my surrounds.
A bow tie and jacket,
On a train to a city of music.
No care of judgement,
No conscience of self.
Purity oozing from old,
Beautifully kept hands;
Blackened fingertips,
Graced with a passion for memories,
Evoked, by such hauntings.
Cradle me, absorb me,
Hold me like a child.
Lose my soul in those memories…
Now all is stopped.

Age 29

Life

Speak to me in a word,
Adrift on melody.
Dance with me in footsteps,
That slide into the ocean.
Speak to me in languages,
So old less forgotten.
Cry with me in raindrops,
That fall into notion.
Sing a thousand laughter's,
That ring through the globe.
Stand a million lifetimes,
The journey cannot be known.   *Age 29*

Warbled

Waters warble in serene symphony,
Peaceful everlasting ripples spread.

Broken trees felled through might unseen,
'O' place of slipping dreams.

Tears of sap cry beneath sultry sky
Fury companions, joyful in play,

Wishing for mind to join their way;
Intoxicated with tormented thought!

Whirling in wonder,
Voice slipping away.

Spell is broken
In a clap of thunder.

Splatting mud, hurried steps:
Rushing, seeking, searching for grip.

Age 32

Heartbreak

No more tears to cry,
Emotions run too high,
Desperation an illusion,
Among the confusion.

Still, hearts beat strong
In the sound of surrender.
Times passed by,
Under the shadows of a starry sky.

Hearts bloom,
From winters gloom;
Fulfil dreams,
In the dance of summer sun.

Paths less trodden, broken.
Still, words should be spoken,
To set free a soul of lost being,
To bring a new beginning.

Age 33

Lost Dream

Still silence creeps asunder, unbeknown.
Still vision is blurred in passions wonder.
Mindless seeking, gloom forsaken,
Eyes engaged; mind lost in wind borrowed tree.

The vanished angel lost in heavens song.
Was it I who trod wrong?
Lamenting on hell's seductive rhyme;
Drifting on the passing of time.

All notions smashed in solitude.
Night to elude misfortunes glance,
Stirring bodies caught in dance,
Simply standing, observing life's lost dream. *Age 33*

Beyond the Dream

Realise it's Alright (Song)

Moon rises high;
Sun sets,
Casting shadows by,
And I sit.

Realise, everything is alright,
Realise, everything is all bright.
All the greens turn to gold.

Moon rises high,
Sun sets,
I wonder why,
I sit,

Dreaming of the times' that we shared,
Remembering how we cared,
Emptiness filled with smiles.

Moon rises high,
I sit,
Watching time drift by,
I cry,

Everything's going to be ok,
Everything is going to be just fine,
I see castles in the sky.

Age 28

Cradled in the Arms of Destiny

Cradled in the arms of destiny,
Where all trials swirl and twist.
Untold truths and imagined illusions entangle.
Believing in the tides and winds of change.
Dancing rays that bloom springs buds,
Sparkle in the dreams ahead.
In struggle, answers are misplaced.
Freedom of letting go,
Rendering change,
No answers;
Only living,
Cradled in the arms of destiny.

Age 29

Eternal Motion

The truest thing is not to believe;
It is not to wish or want,
It is just to be, in this moment,
Completely.
It is all there is, or has ever been;
The real eternity is now!
Moments in time do not pass,
Clocks do not really tick;
Present is eternal motion.

Autumns Hour

Autumns waking hour,
Churning emotions on winds of chill,
Breath without purpose;
Love without onus.

Honesty hidden,
Pursed lips a clue,
Wonder and passion
Slipping gently through,
Hands of softness.

Driving force, just that,
Depleted fatigue,
Loves miracle back to seed,
But to sow? To sow!

Age 33

Young Girl

I used to know a young girl,
She was trapped inside her soul,
Longing to know true happiness,
She let go of it all.

Looking to learn and free her spirit,
She flew through rainbows,
And slept in the clouds,
Danced in the trees,
And stomped on the ground.
The rhythm of her heartbeat, pounding,
Synchronised with the earth.

She said goodbye to everything,
All of her most beloved,
Leaving betrayal and loneliness,
She walked and smiled open hearted.

So many lessons learnt,
As she dawdled without care,
But there was loneliness;
A longing to share.

So, when she thought a daydream came true,
She believed; this was the man she knew.
In truth, even though she was still learning,
Her spirit was captured again.

The rainbows dissolved,
And her clouds turned to stone,
After three long years,
She realised it was time to go it alone.

So, this woman, so close to my life,
Needed to listen more closely to her strife;
Needed to listen to that voice inside,
Know it's her friend,
Not a force to hold her aside,
But a voice longing for freedom.

So, let her keep learning, spirit to run free,
And she'll fly through the rainbows,
And sleep in the clouds;
She'll dance in the treetops
and stomp on the ground.
Let the rhythm of her heart, beat,
Synchronised with the earth.
She'll never stop learning,
Each day is rebirth.   *Age 32*

The Wish

Destiny Walks in Your Hand

Destiny walks in the palm of my hand,
It told me!
But, when I look it's just not there,
All I see
Are swirls and creases.
Birds fly above me,
What's to become of me?
I just don't know.
Where did the sea go?
Tide is out now,
Looks like what's inside my head!
See reflections in the messy seabed,
Reminds me of the life I've led.

Destiny walks in the palm of your hand;
Where else could it possibly stand?
Don't look for it, all you'll find,
Are swirls and creases and a stunning hand.
Destiny walks in the palm of your hand,
Just relax with it;
It walks beside you wherever you go.
There's no destiny without your decision,
Carry it wisely,
Where will you go?
With destiny in the palm of your hand.

Age 33

Dark Fairy

Dark fairy of the moon,
Your knowledge can't come too soon.
Seduce the Earth with your power,
Drawing tides to your beckon and desire.
Be the running waters in the rivers and streams;
Flow through to all hopes and dreams.
Awaken humanity in a moment of time,
Open each soul, so that they may fly.
Let gentleness and peace blow freely in the winds,
Let humanity transcend from material,
To find peace and joy as it begins.

Age 26

Clouds Fulfil Dreams

Silence drifts on a cloud;
Blanketing the chatter of the mind.
In a simple dream of awakening,
Knowing the footsteps ahead,
Though sight is diminished
In heavens deception.
Trust in knowing,
As clouds fulfil dreams!

Age 32

Warrior and Poet

A warrior walking among the trees
Sees a spectacle quite out of ease
Twirling cerise
Beneath a pink blossom tree,

Dancing blushing swirls,
Freeing her sorrow.
Needing to escape, just for a day
She barley glanced up as he came her way.

Mesmerised at the spectacle
This warrior's heart did melt.
There were to be no battles today for our hero
Only this poet's way to dance and play.

She spoke in softness of pain and of joy
He listened and enjoyed her words
But his mind was plagued by the socks he wore;
She thought little, just wanted to soar.

Later their meetings did prove a little strange
A poet's ears offended by a warrior's tales;
Yet there was something between them
Not quite of this world.

Every poet needs a warrior for balance and joy!
Though light and playful, melancholia drenches a poet's soul.
A warrior needs a poet to romance their heart
Nurture their softer side, which can be starved!

And so, this warrior and poet
May seem to some like an unlikely match
But in nature there is always balance
And so is true of hearts.

Age 39

Balance in Darkness

Our boy is lost

Everywhere do I see him,
An imagined vision so very real.
Blinked away in a tear drop.
A wish beyond all wishes,
For our baby boy has gone.
The present has lost perspective,
As days and nights cycle on. *Age 36*

The Drama

Does the drama disguise the pain
And fear of reality?
Is it in the whirlwind,
Where we can ignore the eye of the storm?

A calm place of never-ending sorrow,
For the lives of our loved ones,
And one day ourselves!

Is it through destruction that some find refuge?

For surely by entering the eye,
And feeling the almighty grief
And startling truth of our fragile, wondrous existence.
Why would we want to cause any more pain?!

It's from within the eye,
Unhappily settled in the calm, empty pain,
That the flying debris of fear and anger
Whisk around in senseless turmoil,
Only harming and destroying,
Rather than loving and enjoying.

Curled up in the eye of an awful storm,
That for reasons unknown finds more fuel.
In the calmness, feeling my sorrow,
Sorrow beyond sorrow, beyond sorrow.

Age 36

Love

I'm tired of standing in these shadows
Waiting for the sun to shine on me.

Asking questions, needing answers,
Meaning over distance,
Cannot reach.

In endings there are new beginnings,
Beginnings in tragedy bring ends.
Ever searching for meaning
In the whirlwind that never ends.

Come to me my baby boy,
Feel my love for you,
Flying through the universe's tides,

In every particle of matter,
Every breath of every cell;
My love courses through to find you,
I hope you feel it's true.

Love and light are all around me,
So, you can see me and feel secure
That your mummy loves you,
more dearly than she's ever loved before.

You are my angel,
Sleeping angel.
Fly with my love forever...

Age 36

Beautiful Hands We Share

These hands that have written a thousand tales,
And wiped away a million tears.
They have crawled out of the darkest holes.
Where demons have ravaged and rampaged a soul.

These hands that have forced pain upon their master,
But shortly after realised their artistry and kindness;
Allowed rhythm and melody to run free,
Energy spun with those fingers has seemed magical at times you see.

Though they have held the sorrow of the universe
And wept with pain and grief.
These hands will take all the pain and sorrow
And put it in a beautiful place.

Where angelic song is all around,
In that moment of being,
Where there is everything and nothing,
And all is love and peace.

These hands could write a lifetime,
And when the darker side of grief sets in,
These hands shall waft it past.
The look of an angel guides me
To feel the exquisite pain of the past.

How can there be anger, blame and destruction?
When a tiny baby is so peaceful and angelic?
Warm angel energy filling a room
With kindness and love.

*How could there be a soul on earth
Who could want to hurt anyone or anything else
When a baby dies?*

*We owe it to all sleeping angels
to be the kindest we can be.
Take off the darker side of pain
Be free in love and compassion again.*

*In times of great trouble
The footsteps taken
Are those that lead to our freedom
Or self-persecution.*

*Alone we must walk in our hearts
On the road our soul's destiny takes,
When pain can wash through you
Yet felt completely.*

*Do we take it to a place of destruction?
Or aid our self-realisation?*

*Whilst we remain here,
We must mourn our losses
With time and care.
Beyond all else, keeping the love we share,
We must keep faith and hope alive.*   *Age 36*

Do Not Compare!

Shall I compare the harshness of winter
To the warm kiss of springs sun?
Ice still bites at the exposed!

Shall I speak of tales of love and family?
The release of the Kraken
Or of all the queen's men who came tumbling down?

Shall I cry you the sorrow
Of a Weeping Willow?
Who may weep until all the winds stop blowing?

Where my baby lies for ever more,
Never to smile or grow or laugh,
Had me hold life and death in the same breath.

Shall I tell you the tale of a mother's pain?
It is born from a place of eternal love and care.
Now, I, eternally changed, find strength to lift such a heavy heart.

Should I whimper at your ankles?
Sob the eternal oceans – surely this cannot be so?
Futile thoughts in the sands of times passing.

So, you may see a glimpse of my sorrow,
A head bow of despair,
But to face each and every tomorrow,

I must not compare!

Age 37

Forward Motion

Goddess 2014

I am a Goddess
I shine and exude light
I struggle with my supreme existence.

I am tested
As all Goddesses are
I am shown the way through struggle.

I have been pained in so many ways:
Bound, chastised, ridiculed and demonised;
And I stand here, edged on a precipice
Ready to fly again!

For my fear will never hold me
I am after all a Goddess!
I embrace my fear
And follow my path with grace.

Let the universe pour all its lessons upon me
And I will open my heart and love!
I stand tall,
I illuminate all I feel,
I am me! *Age 37*

Wonderful Hero

Stay where the sunshine's
Where everything is warm,
Relax in the moons glow
With you, I dance in the snow.

My heart is in tatters
As is my mind,
But with you walking beside me
It's a gentler ride.

Even dark times aren't lonely
You help bring happiness into my life.

Dance in the rainbow
Where tear drops shine hue,
I'll never lose you
You're all that is true.

We came together
Through dark forests of pain
But we'll hold hands tightly and dance in the rain.

For you…
You are my hero
And you…
You are my guiding light.

For every tomorrow,
We'll face with our shared sorrow
And dance with joy…. For this is our life.

*Life is sure to crash you down
But it's a choice to wear a frown,
So, take what you can
Love and peace for all human;*

And I'll… I'll walk with my man!

*So, stay where the sun shines
Where everything is warm
For now, that I've found you
I'm not lonesome any-more.* Age 37

To my beloved Carl, without you I would not have got through the last two years. Your love, loyalty, strength, respect and joy have been my salvation. I love you with all my heart as I know our Angel Oscar does too. I can't wait to be parents with you again soon. X

Amelie

A special little girl was born unto me,
whose smile is like a sun beam,
warm and free.
She's a blessing to the world,
her gifts of laughter and joy
spread to all who glance.
Nothing she likes more
than to have a little dance;
a symphony of loveliness and mischief.
Happy as can be.
A gift to the world
for she radiates love and glee.
She is our little sun beam
Amelie X

Age 39

Ripple

"What's around the corner?"
whispered the rivers ripple
to the rushing tide.

"It's the secret discovered though times true course."
"But" the ripple muttered,
"I don't understand time!"

The tide enveloped the ripple into the running river
"Tis the unknown journey little one,
be at peace and flow with me."

Age 39

Sunday Breakfast

Carefree, carelessly being!
Abandoned surrender
Light-hearted and unashamed
Still motion, engaged mind.

Shooting star dust
Happiness abounds.

Love oozing, seeping over land
swept up in the breeze
carried across the sands.
Calmness and fluid ink
longing to flow
to find paper to glide.

Mind to shed wonder
Ponder inner beauty
opened like a flower bud to shine.

Reason undefined or needed
A dance of pen and soul
searching existence and solidarity.

Emerging the butterfly in sunshine of divine presence
What a gift to behold!

Age 40

Symmetry

And the Universe saw me as its own reflection,
looking back on itself, it calms.
Tides drift as they're supposed to,
winds calm and storm with the seasons.
And as the Universe understands
How it feels to gaze upon one's self,
The Earth calms!

Awakening and realisation flood all lands.

And I saw the Universe as my own reflection,
feeling the mystery and mastery of ebbs and flows;
the music of moments,
symmetries in dreams
permeate deep.

Gazing at the Universe
Let us give each other piece?!

Final Note

Sometimes it can seem as though there are no happy endings to a story, but there is always hope; and it's always worth remembering that stories never truly end! They continue beyond the final words written on a page. They are retold, embellished, treasured and loved.

Events happen in life, like the seasons; ever changing, ever challenging. The purpose is simple, because the earth is turning and we're alive! Life was never meant to be easy or pain free, it's always in balance and a rich textured tapestry. Some people have it a lot worse than others, but pain is personal and relative. There is the most beautiful quote that is so true. I'm not sure who wrote it and I hope they don't mind me quoting them!
'Life is not about waiting for the storm to pass,
it's about learning to dance in the rain.'
Words that are all too true and some of the most beautiful moments in life are when we do literally dance in the rain.

We have evolved as a species by adapting, picking ourselves up and beginning again, finding new ways and that's what we must continue to do in a positive, loving and compassionate way; Loving creature and earth alike. No matter what pain we may suffer as long as we're here, standing on Planet Earth staring at our majestic sky and breathing, know there is always hope... eventually... and remember to enjoy as much as you can from where ever you can, as often as you can. It's remarkable that this planet inhabits life in amongst a universe of pure elements and chaos! We are all blessed to walk upon such a magnificent planet, we should nurture and cherish every second we can; for some of us don't even get one day to see our wondrous sky!
Look up, look out and smile!

Peace and blessings to all.
Thank you for reading.

CPSIA information can be obtained
at www.ICGtesting.com
Printed in the USA
BVHW030853160320
575129BV00001B/30

9 781982 238520